"I heartily recommend this workbook! Gina Biegel has crafted a series of mindfulness practices and reflections that are easily accessible, inviting, and wise. Teens who take the time to 'work' this workbook will gain insights about mindfulness, stress, and the mind-body connection that should benefit and serve them for years to come."

—Jeff Brantley, MD, director of the Mindfulness Based Stress Reduction Program at Duke Integrative Medicine and coauthor of *Five Good Minutes® in Your Body*

"This book is an incredible resource for teens, parents, and therapists. It offers easy tools any teen can use."

—Lara Honos-Webb, Ph.D., author of *The Gift of ADHD* and *Listening to Depression*

"This workbook is an excellent resource for any teen dealing with the sometimes overwhelming stress of daily life in the twenty-first century. By using these short, simple practices, readers will discover the natural power and peace that is always inside of them. This discovery will help them deal more successfully with common challenges experienced in school, extracurricular activities, and relationships, and help them to live happier, more fulfilling lives."

—Amy Saltzman, MD, creator of *Still Quiet Place* CDs and courses and director of the Association for Mindfulness in Education

"This workbook is a gift for teens. It offers both mindfulness instruction and stress reduction techniques in a language teens will relate to. The thoughtful exercises and clear instruction are sure to help teens navigate their turbulent years with wisdom and self-compassion."

—Diana Winston, director of mindfulness education at the University of California, Los Angeles Mindful Awareness Research Center and author of *Wide Awake: A Buddhist Guide for Teens*

"Recent neuroscience research suggests that learning to cope with stress actually expands prefrontal brain regions that are important for regulation of emotion and resilience. Biegel's method of using mindfulness skills may be the type of intervention that enhances the development of brain systems important for emotion regulation, and may help to inoculate the adolescent brain against the negative effects of stress during this critical developmental period."

—Amy Garrett, Ph.D., neuroscientist in the department of psychiatry at Stanford University School of Medicine

the
stress reduction workbook for teens

mindfulness skills to help you **deal** with stress

GINA M. BIEGEL, MA, LMFT

Instant Help Books
A Division of New Harbinger Publications, Inc.

Distributed in Canada by Raincoast Books

Copyright © 2009 by Gina Biegel
    Instant Help Books
    A Division of New Harbinger Publications, Inc.
    5674 Shattuck Avenue
    Oakland, CA 94609
    www.newharbinger.com

Cover design by Amy Shoup
Illustrations of meditation poses by Julie Olson

Printed in the United States of America

Library of Congress Cataloging-in-Publication Data

Biegel, Gina M.
 The stress reduction workbook for teens : mindfulness skills to help you deal with stress / Gina M. Biegel.
   p. cm.
 ISBN-13: 978-1-57224-697-3 (pbk. : alk. paper)
 ISBN-10: 1-57224-697-9 (pbk. : alk. paper) 1. Stress management for teenagers. 2. Stress in adolescence. 3. Stress (Psychology) I. Title.
 BF724.3.S86B54 2009
 155.5'18--dc22

               2009044371

17   16   15

15   14   13   12   11

I would like to dedicate this book to all teens who persevere in life. I hope it provides one of the many steps for you on the path to happiness, peace, and clarity. I wish to thank all of my clients, friends, family, and colleagues who have contributed to my creating this book. In particular, I wish to thank Jon Kabat-Zinn, who has shaped my teaching mindfulness with teens.

—Gina Biegel

contents

* contents

introduction

Dear Reader,

Welcome to *The Stress Reduction Workbook for Teens: Mindfulness Skills to Help You Deal with Stress*. Dealing with the stress of being a teen can be very hard, but stress is a normal part of life and you are not alone in experiencing it. Often people are stressed and don't really know what they can do about it. After you work through the activities in this book, you will have a wide range of tools to help you manage stress.

If you're like many people, you find it easy to look at your negative qualities or feel there is no way to fix your problems or stress. This book is about building on the resources, skills, and positive qualities that you might not even realize you have. It is a way to move from "I'm powerless" thinking to "I can do it!" thinking.

Hundreds of teens in stress reduction classes have used activities like the ones in this book, and here is what some of them have said:

- "I learned how to deal with my stress differently, which in the end has helped me stop cutting. I know it was my choice to stop, but the skills gave me ideas to [try] instead of cutting, different ways to calm myself."

- "I have learned to let things go and move on from bad experiences."

- "I felt that the coping skills learned are easy enough and effective enough to be used when I need. I now feel at the very least that I have the ability to reduce my stress."

- "I learned new and different ways to stay relaxed and how to deal with stress and now I don't worry much."

The best way to use this book is by working through the activities from start to finish, because each activity builds on the ones that precede it. If you come to an activity that doesn't fit you or seems odd, you can move on, but it's a good idea to try it first. Also, a number of the activities are mindfulness meditation skills that you can use over and over again, whenever you find yourself stressed.

Congratulations on taking steps to reduce your stress!

Warmly,

Gina Biegel

getting started: setting intentions 1

It's likely that you are often told what to do, whether it's, "Write an essay by tomorrow" or "Take out the garbage." You might even be reading this book because someone suggested that the activities would help you. But even if someone else wants you to complete these activities, you are the one who will work through them for yourself, and figuring out what you want to get out of this book needs to come from you.

What intentions or reasons can you see for learning to manage your stress? Think about your own reasons, not the reasons others have given you. For example, you might think that reducing stress will make your headaches go away or help you sleep better at night. You might think you could communicate better with your friends and family if you were more relaxed.

Write your own goals here:

_____

_____

_____

_____

_____

something more

Now that you have created a list of goals, let go of them. You do not have to strive to accomplish them. Just begin these activities with an open mind and the thought that you might learn something interesting and helpful.

What do you think of the idea of not striving to accomplish a goal?

_____

_____

_____

Have there been other times in your life when you felt you didn't have to strive to accomplish something? Tell about one of these times.

_____

_____

_____

_____

_____

_____

_____

_____

learning who you are 2

At this time in your life you are most likely going through the challenging process of figuring out your identity or who you are while trying to be the person your friends and family want you to be. This is likely to cause you additional stress. The more you learn about who you truly are, who you want to be, and what is most important to you, the better equipped you will be to cope with stress that comes from trying to meet others' expectations of you.

You can begin to learn more about who you are by asking yourself, What is my purpose? What is important to me in my life right now? Of course, each person will have different answers, but these sample responses can start you thinking:

- spending time with my friends

- spending time with my family

- being in a relationship with a boyfriend or girlfriend

- working hard at school

- spending time on my hobbies

- getting better at a sport

- learning a new musical instrument

- taking dance classes

- expressing my thoughts and feelings through writing or drawing

- following my dreams

- figuring out my future

Use this diagram to help you look at yourself. In each blank circle, fill in something that expresses your purpose. Your entries can be as simple or complex as you like. For example, you might write "spending time with friends" or you might just write "friends."

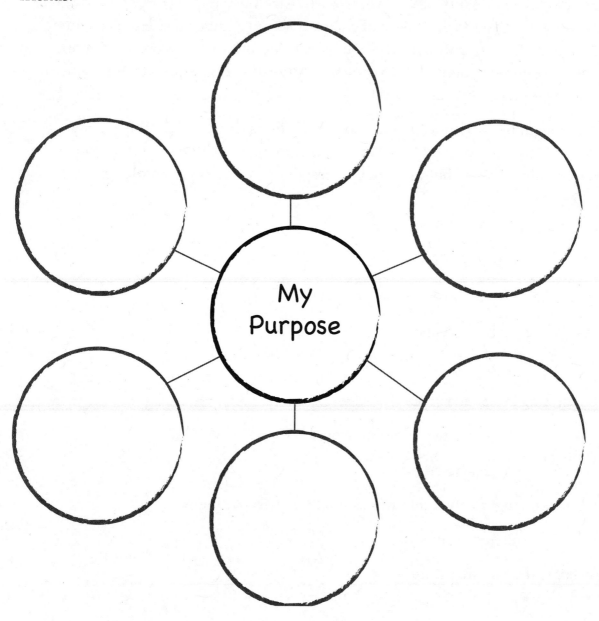

Is your purpose mostly about one area of your life? Or is it a balance that includes such areas as school, career, family, friends, and relationships, among others?

_____

_____

Did you come up with anything you had not thought of before?

_____

_____

Do you want to change any part of your life? If so, what?

_____

_____

_____

Of the parts that you want to change, which can you change? Which parts are out of your control?

_____

_____

_____

something more

How do your friends and family see you? On a separate piece of paper, draw a similar diagram and give copies to a few of your closest friends and family members. Ask them to fill in the circles to describe how they see you.

How are your friends' views of you similar to your own?

_____

_____

_____

How are they different?

_____

_____

_____

Would you like your friends to see you differently? If so, what would you want them to see differently?

_____

_____

_____

_____

How are your family members' views of you similar to your own?

_____

_____

_____

How are they different?

_____

_____

_____

Would you like your family members to see you differently? If so, what would you want them to see differently?

_____

_____

_____

_____

3   defining stress

When someone says they are stressed, you generally know what they mean, but people actually define stress differently. Some people explain it as an uncomfortable emotion, some refer to physical sensations, and some focus on how it affects their thinking.

Here are some words people use to define stress in emotional terms:

- apprehensive
- unhappy
- uncomfortable
- freaking out
- out of control

- overwhelmed
- nervous
- worried
- lost or confused
- wound up

- depressed
- anxious
- frustrated
- overcommitted
- stretched too thin

Here are some words people use to define stress in physical terms:

- tension
- panic
- aches and pains
- chest pains

- headaches
- jitteriness
- trouble breathing
- trouble sleeping

- stomachaches
- dizziness
- excessive appetite
- no appetite

And people might use these words to define stress in terms of their thoughts:

- overthinking
- being in a negative state of mind
- being unable to focus on anything else
- not being able to concentrate

- blanking out on things
- constantly thinking about something
- having bad thoughts
- exaggerating things

- having too much to think about
- having trouble thinking
- having too many things to do

Have you ever used any of these words to define stress? Write them here.

_____

_____

_____

_____

_____

What other words have you used to define stress that are not listed above?

_____

_____

_____

_____

_____

_____

something more

When you find yourself using the words you just listed in your day-to-day life, it is a red flag that you are stressed. Look at your current level of stress and answer these questions:

How is stress playing a part in your life right now?

_____

_____

_____

Do you want the amount of stress in your life to change?

_____

_____

_____

What things in your life are the most stressful?

_____

_____

_____

Which of these things can you change?

_____

_____

_____

good stress and bad stress 4

You probably think of stress as bad or negative, but there are times when stress actually helps you.

Andrew plays soccer on his school's team. He tends to get really nervous before a game, and his stomach often feels a little queasy. At the same time, his adrenaline increases and that helps him perform better.

If you go beyond that perfect point, the balance tips; the stress gets too great. It begins to decrease your ability to do well and starts to hurt you.

Samantha tends to put school assignments off until the last minute. Sometimes waiting close to the deadline works in her favor; she gets her homework done, and the pressure helps her do it well. At other times, she waits too long and the stress is so great that she can't finish her homework and she gives up altogether.

These additional examples will help you see how the balance can tip.

You get named captain of the basketball team.

Good Stress: You are proud of this position and work harder and do better on the team because of it.

Bad Stress: You get so nervous that you start to play worse.

You get a really difficult homework assignment.

Good Stress: You feel challenged by this assignment and spend extra effort on it because you want to do well and are interested in the topic.

Bad Stress: You are so overwhelmed that you give up and don't even do the assignment.

Tell about a time when stress helped you perform better or increased your motivation.

_____

_____

_____

_____

_____

Can you think of a time when you passed that perfect point of stress so that it actually began to hurt you? Describe what happened.

_____

_____

_____

_____

_____

_____

something more

There may be times when you could use stress to your advantage but aren't currently. Can you think of times when stress could help you in each of these areas?

At school: _____

_____

_____

At home: _____

_____

_____

In your hobbies: _____

_____

_____

With your friends: _____

_____

_____

Other: _____

_____

_____

5 the physical effects of stress

When you feel threatened, your body automatically triggers what is called the fight-or-flight response. If you were a caveman hunting for food in prehistoric times and a saber-toothed tiger came into your path, your body would prepare to fight the tiger or to flee from it.

Fortunately, you won't run into a saber-toothed tiger these days. But your body responds to almost every stressful moment in your life with the same response, as if you were encountering lots of tigers every day. For example, a bad grade on a test, a breakup with a girlfriend or boyfriend, being followed on the street, or being startled by a noise when you're home alone can all cause your body to respond immediately with the fight-or-flight response.

Different people feel stress in different parts of their bodies. For example, you might find it harder to breathe, and your friend might feel really warm. Your reaction may also change at different points in time. One stressful situation might give you a stomachache, and another might make your shoulders tense. No matter what your physical signs, be aware that your body is letting you know that it is stressed and wants to return to a relaxed state.

Look at the diagram on the next page. The reactions listed on the left take place as your fight-or-flight response is triggered. After a while, these physical effects go away and your body goes back to a relaxed state, as shown on the right. On this diagram, mark where on your body you generally feel your stress.

Fight-or-Flight Response

⇧ Heart rate

⇧ Pulse

⇧ Blood pressure

⇧ Muscle contraction/
    tension

⇧ Shallow chest
    breathing

⇩ Blood vessel size

⇩ Digestive action

⇧ Body temperature

Relaxed State

⇩ Heart rate

⇩ Pulse

⇩ Blood pressure

⇩ Muscle contraction/
    tension

⇧ Deep abdominal
    breathing

⇧ Blood vessel size

⇧ Digestive action

⇩ Body temperature

something more

The physical effects from the fight-or-flight response (such as your heart beating faster, your breathing becoming heavier, and your body temperature rising) are generally pretty short-lived. However, over time, stress has other effects on the body.

Here is a list of physical symptoms that can be caused by stress. Some of these may last a few minutes or come and go, while others may last for days or even longer. Circle the symptoms you get when you are stressed. If you experience other physical problems that aren't listed, write them in.

asthma	change in sleep habits
stomachache	change in skin: dryness, itchiness, rash
nausea	chest pains
heartburn	dizziness
muscle tightness	throat feels like it is closing
sweating	shortness of breath or shallow breathing
trembling	heavy or faster breathing
headache	racing or pounding heart
change in appetite	other: _____
unusually rapid speech	other: _____
change in weight	other: _____

At times you might not even notice the physical signs that you are stressed, or you might ignore them. But it is important to pay attention when your body is waving a red flag to tell you that you are stressed. It is a sign that you might need to change something in your life to get back to baseline or a more relaxed state.

the emotional effects of stress

When you're feeling strong emotions—especially negative ones—there's a good chance that stress is involved. Stress might cause you to feel depressed or worried. It can affect your behavior, perhaps causing sleeplessness or nail biting. It can even lead to such harmful behaviors as smoking or drug use.

Look at this list of feelings and think about which ones you have experienced in connection with stress. In the clouds on the following page, write down those feelings, or any others you may have had when you were stressed. If you need more room, write your other feelings around the clouds.

angry	hostile	restless
anxious	jumpy	sad
depressed	nervous	suspicious
fearful	numb	worried
frustrated	overwhelmed	worthless
hopeless	panicky	

Take a moment to reflect on what you see. You may have written down just a few feelings or so many that you are upset just looking at them. What thoughts and feelings are coming up for you right now?

_____

_____

_____

Now focus on the positive and notice all the feelings from the list that you haven't experienced as part of stress.

something more

In the outline below, color the parts of your body where you feel emotional pain. Try using different colors to help you express your moods and feelings.

Looking at what you just drew, how do you feel now?

_____

_____

_____

_____

_____

Is there something you drew that you would like to be different?

_____

_____

_____

_____

Did you learn anything new about yourself?

_____

_____

7   thoughts and feelings

What you think affects how you feel. If you generally look at the positive side of situations, it is likely that you will feel happier and more relaxed. But if your thoughts tend to be negative, you will probably feel more stressed.

But what if a negative thought was just a thought and nothing more? You may be giving more power to your negative thoughts than you need to. What if when you thought something you didn't add to it and just noticed what was coming up for you?

In the middle of doing her homework, Diane thinks that no one likes her.

A thought as just a thought

Diane notices herself having the thought that no one likes her and continues to do her homework.

Adding more to the thought than she needs to

Diane stops doing her homework. She begins to think about all the times in the past that she lost a friend. She also thinks about her current group of friends and assumes that she knows what each person thinks of her. These thoughts support her original idea that no one likes her. She starts to feel sad and tired.

The best thing you can do when you have a negative thought is to just notice it instead of adding to it. Can you think of a time when you added more to your thoughts than you needed to? Tell what happened.

_____

_____

_____

_____

_____

Adding more to a thought than you need to can lead to feelings that bring you down. For example, when Diane kept thinking about friends she had lost, she began to feel sad and tired.

What were some feelings that went along with the thoughts you just wrote about?

_____

_____

_____

_____

_____

something more

Try expanding your feelings vocabulary.

Words of anxiety

I feel worried, anxious, afraid, threatened, cautious, hesitant, distrustful, embarrassed, freaked out, and uneasy.

Words of happiness

I feel excited, joyful, stoked, lucky, satisfied, pleased, hopeful, relieved, delighted, and cheerful.

Words of sadness

I feel bummed out, depressed, unhappy, disappointed, hurt, hopeless, lonely, miserable, negative, lost, crushed, and helpless.

Words of anger

I feel mad, bitter, annoyed, irritable, impatient, aggressive, frustrated, vengeful, and enraged.

Choosing from the lists above, what feelings have you had today?

_____

What thoughts come up when you think of each of these feelings?

_____

_____

_____

What feelings words do you most often use to describe yourself?

_____

the mind-body connection 8

Recognizing how your mind and body are connected can give you information about your stress level. Peyton's story shows this connection:

Peyton was supposed to go home right after she got out of school; instead she arrived two hours later. When she walked into the house, her mom and dad both started to yell at her for being late. They accused her of being with her boyfriend when she wasn't supposed to be.

She started to get really warm all over her body, and tears formed in her eyes. She thought, "There's no point in trying to talk to them; they'll never hear me. They don't trust me. They didn't even ask why I was late." She was sad and angry.

Peyton began to yell back at her parents and then started to cry. Finally she said, "I had to take the bus home because my ride left without me and I took the wrong bus home. I tried calling home but no one answered the phone."

To look at the connection between your mind and body, you can use this approach.

Describe the situation:

My best friend decided she did not want to be friends with me anymore.

Look at your thoughts about the situation:

What did I do wrong? I must not be a good friend. Maybe I won't have friends anymore. Maybe my other friends will stop liking me. I am really unpopular. Everybody hates me!

Look at your feelings:

I'm sad, upset, angry, and frustrated!

Notice how your body is affected:

My shoulders are tense. I have tears in my eyes, and my body temperature must be rising because I can feel my face getting red.

Now try it yourself. Describe a situation that you find particularly stressful at this moment.

_____

_____

_____

When you think about this situation, what thoughts are coming up for you?

_____

_____

What feelings are coming up for you about this situation?

_____

_____

How is your body affected?

_____

_____

Do you feel you are responding well to the situation, or are there things you would like to do differently?

_____

_____

You might not know the answer to the last question yet, and that is all right. As you learn more about reducing your stress, this question will be easier to answer.

something more

As you learn skills to manage your stress, you are becoming better equipped to handle whatever comes your way. The result will be a less stressed, more balanced you.

Can you think of a time when you handled a stressful situation really well? Tell what happened.

_____

_____

_____

What might have happened if you had faced this same situation when you were angry?

_____

_____

How would you have known you were angry?

_____

How might you have responded if you were sad or depressed?

_____

_____

How would you have known you were sad or depressed?

_____

You probably know what signals your mind and body give when you are angry or sad and depressed, but you may not always pay attention to them or even really notice them. Tuning into these signals will give you information that can help you start doing things differently.

9 what is stressing you out?

Something that causes you stress is called a stressor. Finding out what your stressors are is an important first step toward change.

Marti works ten hours a week in addition to being in a musical at school and taking a few honors classes. She doesn't know how she'll be able to manage it all. By the time she gets home from either work or rehearsal, it is nine o'clock, and she still has three hours of homework to do. To make things even worse, her friends are mad because she isn't spending a lot of time with them.

· · · · ·

Nathan is upset because his best friend and his girlfriend want him to choose between them. He would like to be able to hang out with both of them together, but when he is with one, he doesn't feel free to include the other. On top of this, his parents are going through a divorce. Nathan also has a lot of trouble with many of his courses, and his father puts a lot of pressure on him to do better in school.

You probably find it easy to see why Marti and Nathan feel stressed. Do you know what your stressors are right now? Circle all that apply to you.

With your friends

peer pressure (sex/drinking/drugs)

appearance or image

relationships in general

competition

problems with a boyfriend or girlfriend

fitting in

drama with friends

In your school life

homework

pressure to do well

bullying

teachers or coaches

grades

pressure about college

sports

classes

Family

parents' financial problems   responsibilities

rules   problems with parents

problems with sisters or brothers   illness

Other

media-generated pressure   finding out who you are   future after school

religious issues   health and fitness   time management

fears   self-confidence   concerns about violence

Use these lines to add something that wasn't listed above or to explain in more detail something you circled.

_____

_____

_____

Sometimes you can't eliminate a stressor completely, but you can minimize its effect on you by spending less time on it or not being so involved with it.

Can you cut any of these stressors out of your life?

_____

_____

Are there others you can change in some way, even if you can't cut them completely out of your life?

_____

_____

something more

Stress is constantly changing. The stressors you just circled most likely will not be the same ones you might circle next year, next month, next week—or even tomorrow. You will resolve some stressful situations, some new ones will pop up, and some will linger for what feels like an eternity.

What stressed you out yesterday?

_____

What stressed you out a week ago?

_____

What stressed you out a month ago?

_____

What stressed you out a year ago?

_____

Which of these stressors no longer stress you out?

_____

Did you resolve any of these on your own? Tell how.

_____

_____

Are you proud of how you handled any of these stressors? Tell which ones, and why.

_____

_____

important moments can cause stress too

Sad or tragic events are obviously stressful. But all kinds of things can cause stress, including events you might think of as positive, such as getting your driver's license or being put into an honors class. Any change in your life—good or bad—has the potential to stress you out.

The events below have been grouped according to the level of stress they are likely to generate for most people. Any single event might be more or less stressful for you, and that's okay. Feel free to shift any event to a different category if you consider it to be more or less stressful.

On the next page circle all of the events you have experienced within the last six months.

Now figure out your score for each of the categories.

Number of highly stressful events you circled x 20 = _____

Number of moderately stressful events you circled x 10 = _____

Number of somewhat stressful events you circled x 5 = _____

Add these three scores to get your total score: _____

Which range do you fall into? Circle it below.

0–20: There are not too many stressful events in your life.

21–80: Your stress level might cause you problems mentally or physically.

81–100: Stress is most likely affecting your life negatively.

101 and up: You are probably experiencing many stress-related problems in your life.

Highly Stressful	Moderately Stressful	Somewhat Stressful	
• Death of a family member	• Use of drugs, alcohol, sex, or self-injury as an escape or way to cope	• Public humiliation	• Achieving or accomplishing something new
• Death of a friend		• Being bullied	• Getting into college
• Divorce or separation of parents	• Sexuality issues	• Having a false rumor spread about you	• Change in sleeping habits
• Loss of a pet	• Change in which parent you live with	• Switching schools	• Friend moving
• Abuse (sexual, physical, or mental)	• Trying to please your parent(s) or live up to their expectations	• Moving	• Trouble with teacher(s)
• Problems with the legal system		• Change in time spent on computer, videogames, and/or phone	• Taking SATs, school achievement tests, or advanced placement tests
• Illness (physical or mental)	• Change in personal or family financial status	• Change in friendships	
• Change of health in someone close to you	• Change in number of arguments with your parent(s)	• Change in number of arguments with friend(s)	• Getting a bad grade
• Pregnancy or abortion	• Trouble with your parent(s) or sibling(s)	• Change in responsibilities at home	• High school graduation
	• Being expelled or suspended from school	• Getting a driver's license	• Increased workload at school
	• Having a new stepparent or stepsibling	• Public speaking	• Taking an advanced placement class
		• Getting grounded or losing privileges	• Grades worse than expected
		• Applying to college	• Trying out for an activity

something more

This score is not meant to freak you out or make you feel bad, but it can help you be aware of what you are facing.

Which of the events you circled are causing you the most stress?

_____

_____

Are any of these events in the process of ending?

_____

_____

Which of these events are out of your control?

_____

_____

Which events could you work on changing to decrease your stress level?

_____

_____

What did you learn about yourself by doing this exercise?

_____

_____

You might want to do this again in the future to see if your stress level has changed.

11 riding the wave of life

Sometimes there are so many stressors in your life that you can almost picture yourself as being in the middle of an ocean wave. Think of this wave as an image for all that is stressing you out right now.

Jon wants very much to please his parents by getting into college. He believes he has to get good grades, play sports, and be in a number of clubs to get accepted. He feels like he has no time for his girlfriend or having fun with his friends anymore. When Jon thinks about his wave, he sees it as a huge tidal wave; he sees himself barely able to stay afloat. He feels like he is drowning out there in the ocean.

■ ▪ ▪ ▪ ▪

Sabrina, on the other hand, finds balance between doing her homework, spending time with her friends, and going to dance classes, which she really likes to do. Sabrina finds that her waves are pretty small, and when they do come through, they are manageable. When her waves get too big, she takes it as a sign that she needs to change something in her schedule. When she does, her waves get smaller again.

Think for a minute about what is stressing you out right now. Imagine translating all of these stressors into the image of a wave. It might be a tidal wave or a very small wave; it is up to you.

In the space provided on the next page, draw a picture of what your wave looks like right now.

List the stressors that make up this wave.

_____

_____

How would you describe your wave: big, small, mean, fierce, calm, mellow, or something else?

_____

What thoughts come up for you when you look at this image and your list of stressors?

_____

_____

What feelings come up for you when you look at this image and your list of stressors?

_____

_____

something more

Even in the strongest of storms with huge crashing waves, the water deep below those waves is perfectly calm and still. Hold in your mind for a moment the image of the wave you drew and try to see the calm below the wave. Write down any thoughts or feelings that come up for you after you have pictured this.

_____

_____

_____

_____

_____

What things have you tried in the past to calm yourself?

_____

_____

_____

Of these things, which ones worked?

_____

_____

_____

Remember to try these things again when you feel that your wave is much too big and you want to drop below into the calm waters.

stepping outside of the box 12

When you were in kindergarten, it's likely that you were told to color within the lines. Since then, people have probably been giving you lots of rules about what you should and shouldn't do. Some of these rules are obviously important. For example, "Don't cross the street before looking in both directions" and "Don't touch the stove burner" serve the purpose of protecting you.

But if you are feeling boxed in by not knowing how to get out of a bad situation or how to solve a problem or by all the advice and suggestions others give you, you can step outside the box (or color outside the lines, so to speak!) and exercise your creativity. This activity will illustrate the point that staying within the lines sometimes limits your ability to see situations from different angles.

Connect these dots using only four straight lines. Do not lift your pencil and do not retrace over any of your lines.

●   ●   ●

●   ●   ●

●   ●   ●

Although you'll find the solution at the bottom of this page, it doesn't matter whether or not you were able to figure it out, and most of the time people aren't able to get the answer. In life, there are often right or wrong answers (and you usually want to be right), but this activity is not about doing it correctly or being right. Rather than trying to get the "right" answer, consider this: Most people approach this exercise thinking that they need to stay within the lines of what they perceive as a box around the nine dots, but that's not what the directions state. This activity and others in this book ask you to see yourself differently than you usually do, to shift your perspective away from the way you see yourself and the world.

In life, do you find yourself staying within the lines or are you able to step outside the box? Explain your answer.

_____

_____

_____

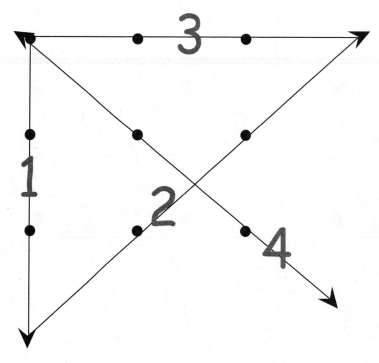

Tell about a situation in which you would like to step outside the box, see or approach a situation differently than you currently are. How can you change what you usually do?

_____

_____

_____

_____

How do people around you respond when you do step outside the box?

_____

_____

_____

_____

In completing Activity 2, you might have noticed that you find it hard to define yourself independent of what others want and expect of you. Write any thoughts or feelings you have about that.

_____

_____

_____

_____

_____

something more

How often do you form boxes around others by judging them with thoughts like, "She'll always be a loser" or "He'll never have any friends"? When you find yourself seeing things this way, keep in mind that you might be harming others—or even yourself—when you judge people.

In what ways have you formed boxes around others by judging them?

_____

_____

_____

_____

_____

_____

How can you remove these boxes?

_____

_____

_____

_____

_____

_____

what is mindfulness?

Have you ever been in bed trying to sleep and repeated in your mind what happened today or yesterday, or what is going to happen tomorrow? We all think about past and future events, but what if you could notice what was happening as it was actually happening in this moment? What would it be like to simply notice your thoughts and your feelings, both physical and emotional as they are right now?

That is the essence of mindfulness, a practice that can help you reduce your stress. Mindfulness is about slowing down, seeing things clearly, and paying attention moment to moment to moment. When you are mindful, you notice what is happening as it is taking place and you are more aware.

To experience mindfulness, sit for a few minutes without doing anything at all—not listening to music or texting or answering the phone if it rings. Just try to notice your surroundings and yourself in this time.

After a few minutes have passed, respond to these questions:

What were your thoughts during this time? What are you thinking right now?

_____

_____

What were your feelings during this time? What are your feelings right now?

_____

_____

What did you notice in your body during this time? What do you notice right now?

_____

_____

There are times when you might not notice what you are feeling, either emotionally or physically, or thinking. For example, you might have had a headache all day and not noticed it until a long time after it had begun. Or you might not have realized you were angry until everything in your backpack fell out and you started to cry over something that normally wouldn't bother you in the slightest.

When you go about your day without noticing how you are doing or what is going on for you, you are missing out on living your life this day, this moment. Being aware of your body, your emotions, and your thoughts right now allows you to be in the present moment. Hopefully, you are more aware and are here instead of somewhere else.

something more

Mindfulness is about paying attention to everything in your life and can help with how you choose to respond to life's situations. The first step toward becoming mindful is learning to just notice what you are thinking and feeling. Instead of responding to these thoughts and feelings immediately, you can begin to sit with them and observe them, before you decide what they mean and how you want to respond. You might still choose to respond the same way, but taking time and space will allow you to figure out how you want to react to a situation, to assess how big or small it is and how stressful it is for you.

Say to yourself, "Oh, this is what I am thinking and feeling right now. I don't have to do anything about these thoughts and feelings. I can just sit with them before I react or make any choice."

What comes to your mind after reading this?

_____

_____

_____

Think of a situation you would like to have responded to differently. What did you do?

_____

_____

_____

If you had taken a moment before you reacted, what would you have done instead?

_____

_____

Before you make a choice about anything you do, you can take a moment to sit with it. There is nothing wrong with taking your time.

14 living in the present moment

Have you ever walked from one classroom to another and not realized how you got there? This is an example of being asleep in your day, of not being fully alive, awake, present, and in the moment right here, right now.

The essence of mindfulness is to bring awareness to everything you do in life. It is in the here and now that you live, and if you are asleep for the day-to-day, think of all you might be missing.

What are you missing when you are focused on your thoughts and feelings about yesterday or tomorrow?

_____

_____

What thoughts, feelings, or worries do you have about things that are in your past and can't be changed?

_____

_____

What thoughts, feelings, or worries do you have about things you think will take place in the future?

_____

_____

When you spend so much time thinking or worrying about what has already happened (things you can't change) or what is going to happen, you are missing out on your life right now!

something more

Close your eyes for a minute and bring your attention to the experience of right now, this very moment. Just be present to what is happening right now.

What thoughts came to your mind?

_____

_____

What feelings came up for you?

_____

_____

What did you feel in your body?

_____

_____

Is yesterday still in your mind? What about last week? Last year?

_____

Is the rest of your day—classes, lunchtime, sports practice—or next week in your mind right now?

_____

Mindfulness is about waking up to the present moment. Would you like to spend more time in the now? If so, when you get stuck in past or future thinking, remind yourself to see this moment. Also, the next activity will help bring you into this moment when you get stuck or are having a hard time being in the moment.

15 being in the now: the five senses

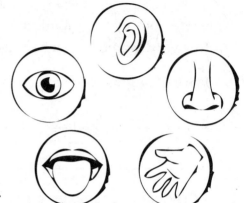

When you were in elementary school, you probably had science lessons about the five senses. Perhaps one of your teachers asked you to close your eyes and try, by tasting or smelling a piece of fruit, to figure out what it was.

Mindfulness is about bringing yourself into the present moment. By using your five senses—sight, sound, taste, touch, and smell—to notice your body and surroundings, you can bring yourself into the now. Try it.

Where are you sitting right now?

_____

_____

What do you see?

_____

_____

What do you hear? It might help to close your eyes.

_____

_____

What do you taste? Can you taste the air? Can you taste your breath?

_____

_____

What do you feel with your hands? With other parts of your body?

_____

_____

What do you smell? Again, you might want to close your eyes.

_____

_____

By using your five senses, what did you notice that you hadn't noticed before?

_____

_____

How are you feeling in this moment?

_____

_____

What are you thinking in this moment?

_____

_____

something more

Here are some ways to do something for yourself, while also using your five senses.

What you see

Make one area of your bedroom neat, without anything cluttering it that stresses you out. Buy a beautiful flower. Go to a museum and observe a piece of artwork that appeals to you. Sit outside and notice nature around you (the sky, the sun, the trees, the stars at night). Look at cool pictures in a book or photographs you or your friends have taken. Notice any of your own drawings that you like. Look at familiar objects (a television, a computer, a cell phone) and find details you hadn't noticed before.

What you hear

Listen to a great song that is soothing or invigorating. Pay attention to the sounds of nature (rain, birds chirping, leaves rustling, waves crashing). Sing a favorite song by yourself or with some friends. Learn to play an instrument, or if you already play, really listen to it. Become aware of sounds you usually hear automatically (the phone ringing, the signal of an instant message, the bell at school).

What you smell

Smell your favorite cologne. Notice the scent of your soap or lotion. Light an aromatic candle and notice the fragrance. Sniff flowers. Smell the outdoors (the grass of the football field, the chlorine of a swimming pool). Pay attention to the smells of food, from freshly baked cookies to garlic and onions. Take a walk in the woods and notice the fresh smells.

What you touch

Notice what it feels like to hug someone or give someone a high five. Put clean sheets on your bed and be aware of how they feel when you first get in. Pay attention to what it feels like to be warm or cold. Notice the feel of your favorite pair of jeans. Feel the warmth of a shower. Touch your pet. Sit in a really comfortable chair.

What you taste

Taste all the food you eat, really taste it. Enjoy every bite of your favorite food. Savor a sweet bite of chocolate. Chew a piece of gum or suck on your favorite mint.

16 mindful eating

People often don't even notice what they are eating or whether they are still hungry. While they are eating, they may be talking on the phone or doing homework or playing around on the computer. What if you just ate and did nothing else for a change? Mindful eating involves noticing how and what you eat, from one bite to an entire meal. By taking time to eat your food, you can begin to learn what foods actually taste like and which ones you like and dislike.

To try eating mindfully, take three raisins. Look at these raisins as something you have never seen before. Before you begin to eat them, notice what is around you in the room and what thoughts and emotions you have. Now notice your breath as you inhale and exhale a few times.

Set two of the raisins aside and take the third in your hand. Look at what you are about to eat. Think about how it got to you, from being a grape on the vine to now being in your hand. Give thanks for what you are about to eat. How do you feel about putting this raisin into your body? How does your body feel, knowing that you are going to eat?

Use your senses to experience this raisin. Notice what it looks like. Roll it around in your hand; what does it feel like? Hold it to your nose; what does it smell like? Place it near your ear; can you hear anything? If you move it between your fingers, can you hear something now?

Feel the raisin against your lips, then lick your lips and notice the taste it has left. Put the raisin into your mouth without chewing it. Close your eyes, if you like, and let it roll around on your tongue. Put it between your teeth and feel it there, without biting into it yet. Notice any saliva that is present. Pay attention to the change in the raisin's texture after it has been in your mouth for a bit.

Bite into the raisin, noticing any tastes you experience. Slowly chew it for as long as you can. Right before you swallow, notice what it feels like to want to swallow this raisin. When you are ready, swallow the raisin. Notice that it is now in your body.

If you notice yourself getting distracted by your thoughts, take a moment and refocus on the raisin. Repeat this process with the remaining two raisins.

You can follow these steps with any food of your choosing, from one bite to an entire meal.

something more

How did the raisins taste?

_____

_____

If you have had raisins before, did they taste different when you ate them mindfully?

_____

_____

Describe how you typically eat—quickly, slowly, and so on.

_____

_____

When the topic of eating comes up, what thoughts and feelings are present for you?

_____

_____

Are there any foods you would like to try to eat mindfully?

_____

_____

What are you going to eat mindfully this week?

_____

_____

17 noticing the little things

There are two types of mindfulness practice: formal and informal. In formal practice, you actually set aside an amount of time and dedicate it to being mindful. Informal practice doesn't require any extra time; the idea is to bring moment-to-moment awareness to everything you already do, to zero in on what you are doing as you are actually doing it.

People often do things without being fully present, as if they were on automatic pilot. Living this way, they cheat themselves out of many moments in their lives. Trying to bring conscious awareness to your body and mind while remaining aware of the task you are engaging in will allow you to experience life more fully. Paying attention to your five senses (sight, sound, touch, taste, and smell) in your daily tasks can help you be aware in the present moment.

Below is a list of some daily tasks that you can bring mindful awareness to:

waking up	walking to class	being with friends or family
brushing your teeth	shopping	
showering	dancing	writing
shaving	riding in a car	journaling
brushing your hair	working out	drawing
getting dressed	folding laundry	playing a musical instrument
tying your shoes	taking out the garbage	playing a sport
washing your hands	washing dishes	getting into bed
eating	cleaning your room	going to sleep

Can you think of any other tasks you do that you can add to this list? Write them here.

_____

_____

Here's an example of how you might bring mindful attention to taking a shower.

Notice the water. Feel the water on your skin and your hair. Smell and taste the water. Smell and feel the shampoo and conditioner in your hand. How do they feel on your head? How does your hair feel when you are rinsing it? If you shave in the shower, notice the shaving cream and the razor; notice how it feels on different parts of your body. Notice when your thoughts move away from the task at hand, the shower, and into the rest of your day, or yesterday or tomorrow. Gently bring yourself back into this moment, to the shower. When you turn off the water, how does it feel? Notice the texture of the towel. How does drying off feel?

Pick another task from the earlier list and bring mindful awareness to doing it.

What task did you choose?

_____

What could you see during this activity?

_____

What could you hear during this activity?

_____

What could you touch during this activity?

_____

What could you taste during this activity?

_____

What could you smell during this activity?

_____

Every time you do this task during the next week, bring mindful awareness to it, using your five senses. Once you feel comfortable doing this task mindfully, try another.

something more

Find someplace where you will not be interrupted. Sit comfortably or lie down, and close your eyes if you feel comfortable doing so. Using your senses to guide you, mindfully listen to your favorite song. If you get distracted by thoughts, gently bring yourself back to the song.

What were your thoughts and feelings listening to this song mindfully?

_____

_____

_____

_____

_____

How was listening this time different from the way you normally listen to this song or to music in general?

_____

_____

_____

_____

_____

doing schoolwork mindfully 18

You can bring mindful awareness to anything you do, including your schoolwork. Follow these steps to help you center yourself before you begin your homework or start to take a test. If you find yourself getting tense or stressed while in the middle of your work, you can repeat this process at any time.

- Get into a comfortable sitting position.

- Place your hands in your lap or on your desk.

- Open your ears to the sounds you notice and allow yourself to be in the room right here, right now.

- Place one or both of your hands on your stomach. Without changing your breath, notice how your stomach gently rises on the in-breath and falls on the out-breath.

- Take five breaths, just as they already are, not trying to change your breaths in any way.

- Notice how your body feels.

- If you feel anxious (or have any other feelings that aren't helpful), take one deep breath. As you release this breath, imagine that you are gently breathing out these feelings.

- Take your next breath and picture ease and peace coming in.

- See yourself taking your entire test or doing all of your homework assignment with ease.

- Imagine yourself gently putting down your pen or pencil when you are done and congratulating yourself on putting forth the effort and doing your best. If you like, you can actually congratulate yourself and even say to yourself that you are intelligent.

You are now ready to begin your test or homework assignment. If you feel stuck, remember that you can take another breath at any time or even repeat the whole process.

something more

Once you have had the opportunity to try this exercise, explain how taking a test or doing your homework mindfully was different from the way you normally do these things.

_____

_____

_____

_____

_____

_____

_____

_____

noticing your body: the body scan meditation 19

This meditation is a formal mindfulness practice that takes you on a tour through your body, from the tips of your toes to the top of your head. When you work on your jump shot in basketball or pitching in softball, you are strengthening your physical skills. In the same way, this exercise can build your mindfulness skills.

There is no right or wrong way to do this meditation; whatever you experience is fine. Allow yourself from ten to twenty minutes for this, and as you get more comfortable doing it, feel free to increase your time. You can set a timer or an alarm so that you don't have to worry about the time. Try to find a comfortable place where you won't be interrupted. If your mind wanders or you notice some physical sensation, like wanting to scratch an itch, don't be concerned. Just kindly remind yourself where you were up to and bring yourself back to that part of the body. Noticing where you are in the moment even when you aren't still on the body scan is being mindful, so compliment yourself on your newfound awareness!

It's likely that you'll need to look at these instructions the first few times you do this meditation. As you get used to doing it, you may be able to do the body scan without having to stop and read the instructions. When you can do that, you might want to close your eyes. Another option is to have a friend or family member read the instructions aloud to you. After you complete the body scan yourself, you might want to read these instructions aloud and lead your friend or family member through it.

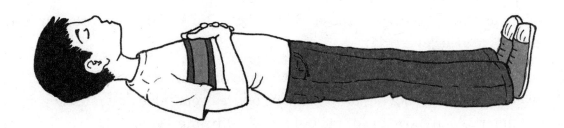

1. Lie on your back in a comfortable position, legs straight and uncrossed and arms at your sides. If it makes you feel more comfortable, put a pillow under your head and/or knees. Close your eyes, if you like. Take a minute to notice the points of contact your body has with the surface you are on, whether it is a bed, a floor, a couch, or some other location. Feel your whole body.

2. Begin to notice your breath, feeling it as it moves throughout your body. Pay attention to where you feel your breath most. You might feel the air as it moves through your nose or mouth. Notice the feeling of your belly rising on the in-breath and falling on the out-breath. Don't try to change your breath in any way; just notice it. As you move through the parts of your body, imagine bringing your breath into each of these areas. If you notice any physical discomfort as you go through the exercise, imagine that you are bringing your breath into the area that troubles you. You can also readjust yourself to get comfortable or stop altogether.

3. Focus on the tips of your toes on your left foot. Try to feel each toe and the spaces between them without moving them. Picture your breath at the tips of your toes. Slowly move your awareness to the bottom of your left foot, to the ball of your foot, then to your heel and what it is in contact with right now. If you can't feel much of anything, that is fine; just notice what it feels like to feel nothing. After a few moments, move to the top of your left foot and ankle.

4. Continue on through your lower leg, your calf muscle, your knee, and your upper thigh; notice all the muscles in your left leg. Try to feel any contact your left leg has with the surface you are on. Once you have reached your left hip, move down to the toes of your right foot and repeat with your right side what you just did with your left side. Once you have reached your hip on your right leg, focus your awareness on both of your legs. Think of the support your feet and legs provide every day.

5. Move your attention to your pelvic area while on your way to noticing your lower back. Slowly moving up your back, notice every bone and muscle you encounter as you move to your shoulders. Breathe into any tension you have in your back or shoulders, taking in fresh air and releasing any tension you have on the out-breath.

6.   Move to your abdomen, again noticing the rise and fall of your belly as you breathe. As you move up to your chest and ribs, try to feel your heart beat.

7.   From there, bring your attention to the tips of your fingers. Try to feel each finger and the spaces between them, without moving them. Pay attention to the air around your fingers and to any contact your hands have with anything else. Notice any sensations in your hands and focus your awareness on them. Move up through your palms and the back of your hands to your wrists, forearms, elbows, upper arms, and shoulders.

8.   Slowly move up to the back of your neck and head. Try to notice the hair on your head. Move forward to the front of your face; notice your forehead, eyebrows, eyelashes, and eyes. Notice your ears, cheeks, nose, mouth, tongue, teeth, jaw, chin, and finally your throat. Pay attention to your nose and mouth and notice where your breath comes in and goes out.

9.   Now focus your awareness on your entire body. Imagine a tiny hole the size of a quarter on the top of your head, like a dolphin's blowhole. Imagine breathing in through this hole, then gently moving the air all the way down through your body and releasing it through the tips of your toes. Slowly breathe in and out like this for a minute.

10.   Notice how you feel at this very moment. To bring yourself back from the meditation, gently wiggle your toes and your fingers. If your eyes are closed, slowly open them when you are ready.

You completed your first body-scan meditation—congratulations! Remember, you can take a piece of how you feel right now with you for the rest of your day.

something more

What did it feel like to just notice your body and breath?

_____

_____

Sometimes people have a hard time being with their bodies. When you think of being with your body, how does that feel?

_____

_____

What physical sensations did you notice?

_____

_____

If you moved or adjusted your body, what was it like to feel the desire to move before you actually moved if you noticed that?

_____

_____

If you felt any physical discomfort, what was that like?

_____

_____

What thoughts came up for you?

_____

_____

What feelings came up for you?

_____

_____

When you got distracted, were you able to gently bring your attention back to your body and breath? What was that like?

_____

_____

If you felt any emotional discomfort, what was that like?

_____

_____

Part of this experience is to just be with all that comes up for you. Everything that arises is absolutely fine. What do you think about this meditation? Was it good, bad, weird, or something else? Did you like it or not?

_____

_____

20 walking meditation: mindful movement

Have you ever walked someplace and not realized how you got there? When you walk to class, to your locker, or to lunch, you obviously get from point A to point B. You might even have a brief interaction with a friend along the way without paying much attention to it. Walking mindfully allows you to use movement to bring yourself into the present moment.

Choose a path about ten feet long; it can be anywhere you will be safe—in front of or behind your house, on the grass, or near your house or school, for example. The overall path doesn't have to be long because you are not trying to get anywhere.

For five to ten minutes, slowly walk back and forth on this path; you can always add to your time later. Move your arms in whatever way is comfortable to you. There is no need to focus on your breathing; just breathe as you normally do. Start to experience what it is like to just walk and notice the sensation of actually walking. Notice what it feels like to lift your foot, step, move, place your foot, and then start again with the other foot. You might want to attend to what causes your leg to lift or what sensations you have in your body. At the end of your path, turn around, paying as much attention to the process of turning as you did to walking.

Your mind may wander while you are walking, and that is normal. When you get distracted, give yourself permission to stop walking. Take a moment to pay attention to the thought, the sight, or whatever it is that distracted you, and then continue walking. What is important is the awareness that you got distracted and started walking again. Each time you engage in a walking meditation, try not to evaluate how you did. There is no good or bad way to do this meditation. Sometimes it will feel great and sometimes it won't, but if it doesn't feel great, that does not mean you did it wrong.

What was it like to walk like this?

_____

_____

Some people are so used to walking at a certain pace that slowing down makes them feel off balance. If you felt off balance walking this way, describe that experience.

_____

_____

What thoughts came up for you during the walking meditation?

_____

_____

If you got distracted, what distracted you?

_____

_____

What feelings came up for you during the walking meditation?

_____

_____

In your daily life, where do you frequently walk?

_____

_____

You can bring this same level of attention and mindful presence to other places where you walk. Even if you can't walk very slowly around some of these places, you can still notice the process of walking, your breath, your body, and where your mind wanders. By increasing your awareness when you walk, you'll be less likely to walk into a classroom and wonder how you got there!

List a few places where you would like to try walking mindfully.

_____

_____

something more

You can bring mindful awareness to a number of different physical activities other than walking. Use your senses (sight, sound, taste, touch, and smell) to guide you in these activities.

During the week, practice bringing mindful awareness to some physical activity you do, and write what your experience is. You can also refer to activity 17 for some examples.

_____

_____

_____

_____

_____

_____

_____

paying attention to your breath: short breathing meditation 21

Breathing is an automatic process. Like your heartbeat, it just happens, most often without your even noticing it. Your breathing is a link between your body and mind, and a fast way to reduce your stress in the moment is to focus on your breath as it is naturally happening, without trying to change it.

Take up to five minutes and just breathe. You can always add more time if you want. If you are a visual person, imagine a picture of an anchor in your chest and think of your breath as the anchor to the present moment. If you get distracted, notice what is distracting you and gently use your breath to bring you back to the present moment. Follow these instructions; it's as simple as 1, 2, 3.

1. **Get in touch with your body.**
    Notice where you are at this very moment. What is around you? Sit comfortably, but try not to slouch. If you feel comfortable doing so, close your eyes. Ask yourself, "What am I feeling in my body right now?" Quickly moving from the tips of your toes to the top of your head, check in with your body, noticing any pains, sensations, or feelings.

2. **Get in touch with your breath.**
    Pay attention to your nose and mouth. Which do you use to breathe in? To breathe out? Notice your belly rising and falling. If you want to, place one or both of your hands on your stomach to feel it. If your mind wanders, gently bring it back to your breath. Just notice and breathe.

3. **Get in touch with what arises.**
    Notice what you are feeling, either physically or emotionally, without trying to change it. For example, you might tell yourself, "I am feeling angry right now. My neck is tense." Notice what thoughts arise, then gently bring your attention back to the breath. Say to yourself, "Breathing in, I calm my mind and body; breathing out, I release all I hold in my mind and body."

something more

After you have tried this breathing exercise, answer these questions.

How do you feel at this very moment?

_____

_____

What was this experience like?

_____

_____

How was it to be with your breath for five minutes?

_____

_____

What thoughts came up for you?

_____

_____

What feelings arose for you?

_____

_____

Describe any discomfort you noticed.

_____

_____

If you were distracted by thoughts, feelings, or discomforts, were you able to return to your breath? How was that for you?

_____

_____

If you were unable to return to your breath once you got distracted, that's just fine. How do you feel now?

_____

_____

If you have difficulty focusing on this meditation, say to yourself, "Breathing in one, breathing out one, breathing in two, breathing out two." Do this for a count of ten, then try the short breathing meditation again. You can also use this count at other times. For example, if you are walking into a tough class at school or about to have a hard conversation with a friend or family member, count your breaths and then continue with your day.

Whenever you do this practice, come to it with fresh eyes. Rather than judging how you did, know that it will be different each time you do it and that just taking some time for yourself is a gift. There is no right or wrong way to practice meditation.

22 sitting meditation: paying attention to your breath and body

The sitting mediation is another formal mindfulness practice, which means that you set aside a specific amount of time to do it. It is based on the short breathing meditation in Activity 21, so you'll want to be comfortable with that exercise before going on to this one. This practice is about noticing yourself in this moment, especially your breath.

1. Find a place where you feel at ease and will not be disturbed. Turn off your cell phone and anything else that might distract you, such as a television, radio, or computer. Choose a position you can comfortably sit in without slouching for ten to fifteen minutes, whether it is in a chair, on the floor, or on your bed. You can reduce or add time to your sitting practice to fit your comfort level.

2. Place your hands and arms either at your side or on your lap, whichever you prefer. You can cross your legs or keep them straight. Once you are able to do this activity without reading these instructions, gently close your eyes.

3. Notice where you are at this very moment. What thoughts and feelings are present? What kind of day are you having? How could what is happening in your day affect this sitting meditation? If you are very distracted and find it hard to sit right now, give yourself the time you need before you begin.

4. When you are ready, briefly check in with your entire body. Notice any physical sensations you have and, before moving on, imagine bringing your breath into any areas that are painful or uncomfortable in your body. Picture yourself breathing in warmth, calm, and peace, and breathing out any tension or pain you hold. Imagine filling these areas with kindness, gentleness, and love if you would like.

5. Begin to feel the physical sensations of just sitting. Notice how your body makes contact with the surface you are sitting on. Bring your awareness to the touch and pressure of this connection. Allow your body to relax into where you are sitting and settle into this moment.

6. Bring your attention to your stomach. Begin to notice how your belly moves as you breathe, how it rises on the in-breath and falls on the out-breath. You can also place one or both of your hands on your belly and feel this motion.

7. Without changing your breath, notice as it moves through your entire body. Bring awareness to your nose and mouth, and notice where your breath enters and leaves your body.

8. If thoughts and feelings arise, just notice them. You might say to yourself, "Oh, this is what I am thinking (or feeling) right now," and guide your attention gently back to your breath. If it helps to bring yourself back to this moment, say to yourself, "Breathing in one, breathing out one, breathing in two, breathing out two."

9. Each time you notice that you are up in your mind or focusing on your to-do list, gently note that this is normal; it is what your mind naturally does. When you come back to your breath and your sitting, congratulate yourself for noticing that you got distracted and have come back.

10. When you are done, slowly move the tips of your fingers and your toes and then bring yourself back into this room. If your eyes are closed, gently let light come back into them. You can bring a piece of this moment and how you are feeling right now into the rest of your day.

Remember, there is no need to judge this sitting meditation as good or bad. Just accept it as time for you to rest with what is.

something more

How did it feel to sit and be with your breath and body for ten to fifteen minutes?

_____

_____

What thoughts came up for you?

_____

_____

What feelings came up for you?

_____

_____

What discomforts arose?

_____

_____

If thoughts, emotions, or physical sensations distracted you, describe them.

_____

_____

How did you bring yourself back to the moment if you did?

_____

_____

People spend a lot of time in their heads, thinking. When you spend so much time thinking, how much time are you living in the now?

When Bailey went to bed at night, she had a very hard time falling asleep. Her to-do list would pop up, and it would take her a long time to get it to go away. When she got up in the morning, she was often really tired.

Learning to observe your thoughts as they arise—without adding to them or trying to push them away—can reduce your stress. This activity can help; you can also use this technique during any of your meditation practices if you find yourself distracted by your thoughts.

Seated in a comfortable position, imagine yourself sitting on top of a hill. Once you have this image in your mind, look down at the bottom of the hill and see a train track. Picture a train starting to pass. As you see each car go by, think of it as one of your thoughts. Without jumping onto the train, notice the thoughts as they pass. If you find that one thought keeps popping back up, just notice it. You can say, "Oh, this is what I am thinking right now" and move on. When you notice you have jumped on the train, gently get back on the top of the hill

Bailey tried this exercise. She found that when she just noticed her thoughts without telling herself, "I need to stop thinking about this or I'll be tired tomorrow," and said "okay, I'm not thinking about this," and just noticed it, it helped her fall asleep without getting stuck in a cycle of thinking on and on.

something more

Draw the train that was in your mind. On the picture of the train, write the thoughts that often come up for you and make it hard for you to relax.

When you notice these thoughts, just let them pass as a train passes by.

Most often, people like to take in the "good" moments and avoid or push away the "bad" moments. Please read this poem aloud or silently two times.

The Guest House

This being human is a guest house.
Every morning a new arrival.

A joy, a depression, a meanness,
some momentary awareness comes
as an unexpected visitor.

Welcome and entertain them all!
Even if they're a crowd of sorrows,
who violently sweep your house
empty of its furniture,
still, treat each guest honorably.
He may be clearing you out
for some new delight.

The dark thought, the shame, the malice,
meet them at the door laughing,
and invite them in.

Be grateful for whoever comes,
because each has been sent
as a guide from beyond.

—Rumi

What do you think this poem means? There are no right or wrong answers; just tell what it means to you.

_____

_____

_____

_____

"Bad" moments help you know that other moments are "good." What does this mean to you?

_____

_____

What feelings are in your "guest house" right now?

_____

_____

When you experience negative feelings, can you just take them in as information for yourself? Tell how you might do that.

_____

_____

How do you currently deal with negative emotions?

_____

_____

Rumi's poem suggests that negative emotions can clear "you out for some new delight." What thoughts and feelings does this up bring up for you?

_____

_____

_____

_____

Can you think of what that new delight could be?

_____

_____

_____

something more

In the space below, draw a picture of a house that represents you right now.

What feelings are present for you?

_____

_____

What thoughts come up for you?

_____

_____

What would it mean to "be grateful for whoever comes"?

_____

_____

focusing on the negative

Part of life is to take in both the bad and good times. People often want to push away or avoid bad times, but if you never had bad times you might not be able to notice good times.

> At school, Rachel tripped in front of some of the popular kids in the quad. In her first class, her favorite teacher called her out for texting in class. She got so upset that a few people laughed at her, which embarrassed her and made her even more upset. She then went to hand in her English essay and realized she had left it home.

Days like Rachel's will happen. Simply noticing when you are having a bad day without adding more emotion or thought to it will make it just a bad day and nothing more.

Notice one unpleasant event every day for the next week and add it to the calendar on the next page. First, tell what the event was. Then describe any thoughts or emotions you experienced before, during, and after the event. Tell what you felt in your body before, during, and after the event. Finally, tell how you feel and what you are thinking right now.

Unpleasant Events Calendar			
	The Event	**My Emotions or Thoughts**	**What I Felt in My Body**	**What I Feel and Think Now**
Example	My friend told my secret to the group we hang out with.	I was worried that the rest of my friends would be mad at me. Afterward, I felt hurt and sad.	I felt really warm and my stomach started to hurt.	I feel like I can't trust anyone and I don't know how to make things right with the rest of my friends.
Monday				
Tuesday				
Wednesday				
Thursday				
Friday				
Saturday				
Sunday				

What was your experience of looking for the negative? Did it make you feel worse or change your mood in some way?

_____

_____

_____

_____

_____

Which of these events resolved themselves pretty quickly?

_____

_____

_____

_____

_____

something more

People don't usually want unpleasant things to happen, but they are a normal part of life. A lot of what makes an event unpleasant has to do with the feelings and thoughts you add to it. The more you try to resist what is or wish for things to be different, the more you make an unpleasant event even worse.

Looking back at these events, did you make any of them worse? If so, tell how.

_____

_____

_____

_____

_____

If some time had gone by before you reacted to these events, might you have reacted differently? Tell how.

_____

_____

_____

_____

_____

letting go of negative self-judgments 26

"I am ugly." "I am fat." "I am stupid." "I'll never make the team." Do you find yourself having thoughts like these? Do you often blame yourself or find yourself unhappy with what is and wanting things to be different? Do you use words like, "I should have" or "I could have"? If your answer to any of these questions is yes, you are listening to an inner voice of negative self-judgment.

Judgment involves assigning some value to situations, defining them as good or bad, right or wrong. You can free yourself from a lot of added stress by learning to let go of your negative inner voice and to accept what is, simply because it is, without judging yourself.

What negative judgments do you make about yourself?

_____

_____

_____

When you notice one of your judgments, follow these steps to shift away from it. Read the examples and then try it yourself.

Step 1: State the judgment.

I am ugly.

Step 2: Notice what makes it a judgment.

"I am ugly" is a judgment because it involves adding a value to how I look. There is no objective way to measure if I am ugly or not.

Step 3: Say to yourself with openness, gentleness, kindness, and curiosity: "Oh, interesting. This is what I am thinking now."

I am thinking I am ugly right now.

Step 4: Notice whether this thought is unusual or if you have a pattern of judging yourself this way.

I tend to say I am ugly a lot.

Step 5: Think of what you could tell yourself instead.

I am not feeling too great today. I don't think I look my best.

Step 6: Thank yourself for noticing the judgment and end with a kind statement about yourself.

Good for me! Noticing when I say mean things to myself is the first step to doing it less often, which is something I deserve.

Step 1: _____

_____

Step 2: _____

_____

Step 3: _____

_____

Step 4: _____

_____

Step 5: _____

_____

Step 6: _____

_____

something more

People don't make negative judgments only about themselves. They also tend to judge others negatively, including people who are close to them and people they don't even like or know.

What are some judgments you have made about family members?

_____

_____

What are some judgments you have made about friends?

_____

_____

What are some judgments you have made about people you don't like?

_____

_____

What are some judgments you have made about people you don't know?

_____

_____

Do you think that judging others negatively contributes to your stress? If so, tell how.

_____

_____

_____

27 helpful and unhelpful ways to cope with stress

Not all ways of coping with stress are helpful. Some people engage in unhelpful behaviors, perhaps thinking that these behaviors will somehow fix their problems. Instead, they find that their problems get worse or that they develop new problems.

A year ago, Brad started having a beer at parties with his friends. He felt like it relaxed him so he began to have a beer or two after a hard day at school. Now he finds that he needs to drink just to get through every day. He steals liquor from his parents and sometimes from the grocery store. His mom just caught Brad sneaking in through his bedroom window, really drunk.

Like most unhelpful behaviors, Brad's drinking has snowballed out of control and become a much larger problem for him.

Put a check mark next any of these unhelpful coping behaviors that you have engaged in during the past three months. If you prefer to note the behaviors in your mind rather than checking them, that's okay.

- ☐ alcohol use
- ☐ drug use, including improper use of prescription drugs
- ☐ smoking cigarettes
- ☐ drinking lots of caffeine
- ☐ distracting yourself by spending a lot of time on the computer
- ☐ isolating yourself by staying in your room more than usual
- ☐ spending less time with your friends or family
- ☐ not doing things you previously enjoyed

- ☐ sleeping more or less than usual
- ☐ having unprotected sex
- ☐ having multiple sex partners
- ☐ cutting yourself
- ☐ burning your body
- ☐ overeating or undereating
- ☐ making yourself vomit after eating
- ☐ excessive exercising
- ☐ stealing
- ☐ getting involved with the wrong crowd
- ☐ getting into fights

List the positives and negatives for the behavior you have engaged in most often (or thought about, if you haven't actually engaged in any of them) from the previous list.

_____

_____

_____

People often notice that the negatives seem to outweigh the positives of unhelpful coping behaviors. What do you think?

_____

_____

_____

Below are some healthy ways of coping with stress. These helpful behaviors don't have any negative effects or lasting consequences unlike the unhelpful behaviors. Put a check mark next to the ones you use or could use. On the blank lines, add any others you can think of.

☐ taking some time away from an upsetting situation

☐ writing

☐ listening to music

☐ drawing

☐ talking or spending time with friends or family

☐ _____

☐ _____

☐ _____

Sharing your concerns with others can help you feel better. Having someone to turn to when you aren't doing well is really important, whether it is a friend, a parent or other relative, or an adult at school.

Who can you share your concerns with?

_____

_____

_____

If you aren't comfortable sharing a particular problem with the people you listed, or you have a problem that seems too big for someone currently in your life to help with, consider speaking with a mental health professional. Your parent, teacher, or school counselor may be able to help you get started.

something more

When you find yourself about to do something that is not healthy for you, try grabbing an ice cube and holding it in your hand until it melts completely. You might also try closing your eyes and counting your breaths (breathing in one, breathing out one, breathing in two, breathing out two) while the ice cube melts.

Holding an ice cube will not make you feel worse after you do it, and it will not add onto your problems, but it can replace what you are trying to get out of an unhelpful behavior.

28 pleasant life moments: doing what you enjoy

There are probably days when you are so busy or upset that you don't take the time to do things you enjoy. On the worst of days, you might even forget that there are things that bring you joy. Or perhaps you are doing these things, but not remembering to notice that they make you happy.

Mira got into a fight with her parents this morning before school. Then she got her algebra test back and she had flunked it. When she got her lunch, she dropped her tray on the floor, and everyone nearby turned to stare at her. She felt like her day was the worst ever!

. . . . .

Brandon got a letter saying that he hadn't been accepted to the college he wanted to go to. He was very upset and was also worried about telling his parents. He wanted to contact his friends for support, but he couldn't. On top of everything, he had been grounded for coming home late last weekend, and his phone and computer privileges had been taken away.

When you have had a bad day like Mira's or Brandon's, it is the perfect time to think of things that bring a smile to your face or make you feel better. If you are down in the dumps, so to speak, you don't have to stay there; you can do something about it.

On the next page is a list of things that can be considered pleasant life moments. Put a check mark next to all the activities you enjoy doing. Then go back and put a star next to your top three.

- ☐ spending time with pets
- ☐ being outdoors
- ☐ writing
- ☐ taking pictures
- ☐ doing a hobby
- ☐ playing or listening to music
- ☐ spending time with friends
- ☐ gardening
- ☐ drawing or painting
- ☐ exercising
- ☐ playing a sport
- ☐ meditating
- ☐ doing yoga
- ☐ reading
- ☐ taking a bath
- ☐ watching movies

- ☐ volunteering
- ☐ eating out
- ☐ going to a sporting event
- ☐ going to a concert
- ☐ camping out
- ☐ traveling
- ☐ talking on the phone
- ☐ texting
- ☐ shopping
- ☐ dancing
- ☐ singing
- ☐ cooking
- ☐ spending time on the computer
- ☐ playing video games
- ☐ spending time with family

Are there activities you enjoy that were not on the list? Write them here.

_____

_____

something more

You might think that you don't have time to enjoy activities like these. But no matter how busy you are, you can do things that are pleasant and don't take a lot of time: for example, noticing the sun or a pretty flower, enjoying the aroma and appearance of what you are about to eat, or appreciating a conversation with a friend. Learning to notice what little things in your life can bring you happiness—and focusing on them rather than on the negatives—will improve your mood and reduce your stress.

Write down the three activities you checked (circled) earlier. Then choose two more and add them.

1. _____

2. _____

3. _____

4. _____

5. _____

This week, try at least two of these activities. After you do each, reflect on whether it made you feel better. Then write what it was like to take the time to do something you enjoyed.

Activity 1

_____

_____

Activity 2

_____

_____

focusing on the positive

29

Most people think they want to be happy and to enjoy their lives, and many express that desire in words. But actually being happy and enjoying your life takes more than just a passing thought or statement; it is about actively noticing and doing what makes you happy.

Olivia was really happy. She was going to get her braces off after two years, and she just found out that she got a B on her biology test, which had been really hard for her. When she left the class, she got a hug from her best friend.

■　■　■　■　■

Nora was excited because her parents had agreed to let her go to a battle of the bands show, where her favorite punk band would be playing. She was content in general because she felt that her friendships were going well, without any of the drama that so often went on.

■　■　■　■　■

Walking home from school, Tristen saw a rainbow and it brought a smile to his face. He had had a so-so day, and seeing that rainbow really made him happy. When he got home, he had a good talk with his brother and found chatting online with friends that night was really fun.

Many people allow one negative event to outweigh the positives of a day, but there are almost always good moments, even on days that might seem bad. You might not always notice these good moments if you are caught up in the negative or too busy thinking about the past or future. Like Olivia, Nora, and Tristen, you just need to look for the good moments and pay attention to the things that made you happy.

Notice one pleasant event every day for the next week and add it to the calendar on the next page. First, tell what the event was. Then describe any thoughts or emotions you experienced before, during, and after the event. Tell what you felt in your body before, during, and after the event. Finally, tell how you feel and what you are thinking right now.

Pleasant Events Calendar				
	The Event	**My Emotions or Thoughts**	**What I Felt in My Body**	**What I Feel and Think Now**
Example	I passed my driver's test.	I was really stoked. I can't wait to drive to school!	I had butterflies in my stomach during the test. Afterward I couldn't stop smiling.	I am still really happy and can see how it is going to change my life.
Monday				
Tuesday				
Wednesday				
Thursday				
Friday				
Saturday				
Sunday				

something more

What if a day could be just a day—not pleasant or unpleasant, not good or bad, but just a day filled with all types of moments? How would thinking this way change your perspective?

_____

_____

Write what comes to your mind when you think of the word "happiness." If you prefer, take a separate piece of paper and draw what comes to your mind.

_____

_____

What is your most recent memory of something that made you happy?

_____

_____

What about you makes you happy?

_____

_____

What things outside of you make you happy, like friends, family, hobbies, and so on?

_____

_____

Why do you think happiness is so important?

_____

_____

What could you do right now or in the near future that would make you happy or happier than you already are?

_____

_____

Think of someone you know who seems happy. Ask what that person thinks happiness is. Write it here.

_____

_____

_____

seeing your positive qualities
30

Many people can list their negative qualities much more quickly and easily than their positive ones, and their negative lists tend to be longer as well. If you view yourself as a valuable person with qualities you like and are proud of, you have high self-esteem. High self-esteem can make it easier to manage stressful moments because you are not likely to complicate situations by adding negative thoughts about yourself.

> *Jon used to see himself only negatively. He would say, "I'm bad at football and I'm really not that smart." He has worked to feel comfortable with who he is and to improve his self-esteem. Now, when he notices that he is thinking negatively, he tries to see the other side as well. He reminds himself that only ten guys from his junior class made the varsity football team and that he has brought up his grade point average from a 2.8 to a 3.3.*

When you find yourself focusing on the negatives about yourself, you can counter it with something positive or realistic like Jon did.

If someone asked you what you think of yourself, what would you say?

_____

_____

In the columns below, list your positive and negative qualities.

Positive qualities   **Negative qualities**

_____   _____

_____   _____

_____   _____

_____   _____

_____   _____

What was your experience doing this activity?

_____

_____

_____

_____

_____

_____

something more

Affirmations are positive statements you can say to yourself. You can use affirmations to talk back to negative thoughts that come to your mind. Here are some examples:

- I am a valuable and unique person.

- I always do the best I can.

- I love myself.

Write five affirmations for yourself.

1. _____

2. _____

3. _____

4. _____

5. _____

What is it like for you to say nice things to yourself?

_____

_____

If you find it difficult to say nice things to yourself, try imagining that you are talking to a friend.

31 self-care versus being selfish

Taking care of yourself is different from being selfish. Selfish people think only of themselves and aren't concerned about others. When you take care of your mind and body, you are not being selfish; you are helping yourself function happily and successfully in daily life. By caring for yourself, you are making it possible for you to be there for others.

Here are some tips to help take good care of yourself:

- Practice the mindfulness and relaxation techniques you learned in earlier activities.

- Set realistic goals for yourself.

- Say kind things to yourself.

- Eat healthy foods.

- Get enough sleep.

- Exercise.

- Turn your negative thoughts into positive ones.

- Have compassion for yourself.

- Ask for help when you need it.

How do you define being selfish?

_____

_____

How do you define self-care?

_____

_____

Which, if any, of the tips given above do you already follow? Which others could you follow?

_____

_____

Whenever you feel that taking care of yourself or making time for yourself is selfish, think twice. Remember this: The heart pumps blood to itself first before the other organs in the body. Similarly, you need to consider yourself before you are able to give to and be there for others.

Fill in this outline with what you imagine your heart is. Is it full or empty? What colors does it contain, what thoughts or feelings? If you find that your heart isn't as you would like it to be, you may need to do more for yourself.

something more

Thermostats balance temperature by turning heating and cooling devices on and off. Imagine that your body gives off information that lets you know when you aren't in balance and then, like a thermostat, takes action to get itself back in balance.

Are you able to notice when your body and mind are out of balance? How can you tell?

_____

_____

What things in your life get you out of balance?

_____

_____

What temperature is your emotional thermostat set at?

_____

_____

How far from that temperature do you need to be before you realize your air conditioning or heat should be on?

_____

_____

If you could control everything that happened in your life, there would be no reason to get stressed out because things would just work out the way you wanted and expected them to. Unfortunately, none of us has that much power, and the things that stress us out are often out of our control.

You undoubtedly realize you can't control certain things, like the weather, how much math homework you get, and what time you have to be at school. Then there are things you can't control, but perhaps think you can, like other people.

> *Molly and Rebecca had talked about shopping together for dresses for an upcoming dance. Molly was really looking forward to shopping with Rebecca, but every time she tried to settle on a day to go, Rebecca had something else to do. The date of the dance was not far away, and Molly was really stressed. Finally, she decided to invite another friend to go with her.*

No matter how much Molly wanted to shop with Rebecca, she could not control what Rebecca did. Once she realized that, she was able to change her actions and reduce her stress.

For each of these categories, list some problems you have had or are now having.

Family

_____

_____

Relationships

_____

_____

School, work, or extracurricular activities

_____

_____

Physical or mental health

_____

_____

Behaviors to escape or avoid life (for example, risky sexual behavior, drug or alcohol use, or self-injury)

_____

_____

Circle the ones you have some control over and are able to change. Cross out the ones you have no control over.

Focusing your effort on the problems you can change is much better than spending energy on the things you have no control over!

What do you think of this idea?

_____

_____

something more

When your friends are stressed by problems, you may find yourself feeling stressed right along with them, but it is important for you to know that your friends' problems are theirs, not yours. Although you will probably be affected by these problems, you cannot control them and taking them on as your own will only increase your stress.

Tell about a problem one of your friends is having.

_____

_____

_____

_____

How does this problem make you feel?

_____

_____

_____

How can you help your friend without making the problem your own?

_____

_____

_____

33 problems: yours and other people's

Are you that friend who always listens to everyone else and never shares how you are doing or feeling? Do you take on everyone else's burdens? Are you the son or daughter who is always making sure your parents are okay?

Susan is always listening to everyone else's problems. She thinks that if she can listen a little longer or do a little more for her friends, their problems will get better. But after hearing everyone's problems, Susan can't sleep at night. She is so worried about her friend Amy, whose parents are getting divorced, that she has started to get headaches and can't focus on her homework. Susan has her own problems to deal with—her boyfriend has just broken up with her and her grandmother is very sick—but she doesn't share her problems with anyone else.

It is great to care about the people in your life, to be a good friend and a good son or daughter, but there is a line between caring and worrying. As much as you might want to and no matter how much you worry, you can't control the outcome of things that are stressing your family or friends. Be a listener, not a worrier like Susan. You can listen to your friends, give them a shoulder to cry on, and be there for them, but don't let their problems consume your life. And when you have a problem of your own, don't keep it all inside; let your friends listen back.

List the things in your friends' or family members' lives that are worrying you right now.

_____

_____

_____

_____

Of these, which can you affect or control by your worrying?

_____

_____

_____

This question is a trick one. You should have written nothing because you can't change anything by worrying. If you understand that your worrying will not change the outcomes of people's problems, you will feel less stressed.

something more

What problems in your own life would you like others to help with or listen to?

_____

_____

_____

Of these, which are you actually sharing and getting help for?

_____

_____

Are you able to trust people enough to let them in?

_____

_____

List the people you trust most and could go to if you feel down in the dumps or need help.

_____

_____

_____

What can you do to be sure you get the help you need, especially if there aren't people you trust?

_____

_____

changing how you cope with painful situations 34

At one time or another, everyone experiences upsetting events, such as a breakup with a boyfriend or girlfriend, failing a class, or not getting a part in the school play. The pain these events cause can be large or small; it can be emotional or physical (for example, a really bad headache or backache).

What you do with the pain you experience in connection with events like these affects your overall level of stress. Often people add onto their pain by blocking it, which will make a stressful situation even worse. Blocking can include:

- denying that the problem exists

- denying the pain it causes

- feeling guilty

- constantly thinking about what happened

- judging yourself

- telling yourself that you should have done something differently

- holding or clinging onto the problem

- resisting or pushing the pain away

The first step in reducing your stress is to notice when you are blocking a painful moment. Then you can make choices to change what you are doing.

Paul's girlfriend Emily just broke up with him. He keeps calling and texting her several times a day, and she doesn't respond to him. When he tries to talk to her at school, she walks away. He keeps thinking about what a loser he is. He tells himself that it is all his fault and that he will never get over her. He is so angry and sad about the breakup that he starts to fight with his parents.

Paul is obviously going to feel some pain, but he can reduce his stress by changing his actions. For example, he can acknowledge that his calling and texting has not made things better, and he can then decide to stop. He can choose to spend some time with friends, which will help him feel better and might improve his mood around his parents. He can tell himself that it's okay to feel upset when he sees Emily at school and remind himself that it will take time to get over that feeling.

Tell about something in your life that is causing you pain right now.

_____

_____

_____

What are you doing to block your painful situation or make it worse? Look at the list on the previous page for examples.

_____

_____

_____

Of those things, which can you change or stop doing?

_____

_____

_____

Can you think of things you often do to block you pain that aren't on the list?

_____

_____

_____

Can you think of other times when you blocked your pain?

_____

_____

_____

something more

In the future, when you encounter a painful situation, ask yourself what you are doing to block this pain. Think about what you can do to change so that you can reduce—or even eliminate—the stress you feel in connection with this situation. Try this out and write about what happened.

_____

_____

_____

_____

_____

_____

_____

mindful stopping: taking time before you react

Have you ever acted in anger and later wished you hadn't? Have you ever spent a lot of time thinking about something that seems so huge only to realize a week later that it wasn't such a big deal? Mindful stopping is a way for you to check in with yourself before you act or react in stressful moments. You can use this practice whether you are about to react to your own thoughts or to someone else's words or actions.

> *Luis loves to play basketball. He sees a group taking practice shots on the playground and he wishes he could join them. He thinks, "They'll never let me play" and turns to leave.*

▪ ▪ ▪ ▪ ▪

> *Destiny always tells herself that she is fat. Then one day at school, another girl calls her a "fat whale" as they are about to pass each other in the hall. Destiny is so angry that she puts out her foot and trips the girl. She ends up in the principal's office.*

Mindful stopping could have helped Luis ask to join the game and prevented Destiny from harming someone else and getting in trouble herself. Here's how it works:

1. Visualize, if you would like, a stop sign. You can also say to yourself, "Stop," in a gentle voice.

2. Check in with your body. Begin with the tips of your toes and move up to the top of your head. Along the way, notice if anything is tight, tense, or just does not feel right.

3. Imagine bringing your breath into the places that feel discomfort. For example, you might have a tight feeling in your chest, and your stomach might hurt. Be aware of your body, and breathe in without changing your breath. If it helps, say to yourself, "Breathing in one, breathing out one, breathing in two, breathing out two," for a count of ten breaths. You can also say to yourself, "Breathing in fresh air, breathing out discomfort."

4.   Take a breath and imagine bringing in air through a small hole at the top of your head. Let the breath move through your body and release it through the tips of your toes.

5.   Ask yourself these questions:

   • How do I feel now?

   • Do I want to react within myself?

   • Do I want to react toward someone else?

   • Am I overreacting?

   • Am I judging myself or others?

   • Do I need some time before I decide what I want to do?

Taking some time will often let you see a situation more clearly. You might make a different choice, which might prevent a problem or avoid negative consequences.

something more

Describe a stressful situation where you reacted without stopping yourself. This situation can be based on a thought you had about yourself or on someone else's actions or words.

_____

_____

_____

How did you respond to this situation?

_____

_____

_____

What feelings were present?

_____

_____

_____

What thoughts were present?

_____

_____

_____

What did you feel in your body?

_____

_____

_____

Now imagine yourself going through the mindful stopping process in the same situation. Are your feelings different? If so, how?

_____

_____

_____

Are your thoughts different? Are you spending more or less time thinking about this situation?

_____

_____

_____

Is your response different? If so, how?

_____

_____

_____

playing out the end of the movie 36

When you are trying to make a decision, it can help to play out the movie. Ask yourself, if this situation were a movie, how would it end? What consequences will your actions lead to?

Some of Kierra's friends were planning to cut class and go to the beach on Friday. It sounded like fun, and Kierra was thinking about joining them. But she had already been caught cutting class three times and had finally regained her parents' trust after promising that she wouldn't do it again. When she played out the movie, she thought about the potential consequences: she might be grounded or lose some privileges, and worst of all, her parents would stop trusting her. Kierra decided not to join her friends in cutting, and she felt really good about her decision.

Think of a time when you made a choice and didn't like the way the "movie" ended. Describe the situation.

_____

_____

_____

If you had played out the movie beforehand, what would you have done differently?

_____

_____

_____

something more

You can't change the past, but you can learn from your mistakes. Think of a situation in your life that you are trying to decide on now. Describe it here.

_____

_____

_____

What choices do you have in this situation?

_____

_____

_____

How would the movie play out with each choice?

_____

_____

_____

Let this guide your decision.

Congratulations! You have been on a journey to learn ways to reduce your stress, and you have worked very hard to get to this point. Commend yourself for trying to better yourself and improve your health.

Now that you have completed the activities in this book, you might be wondering about what to do next. The best way to continue to manage your stress is to spend time on the mindfulness practices you have learned. You can use the informal mindfulness practice—bringing mindful attention to everything you already do in life—so you don't have to spend any extra time. When you have more time, do some of the other practices, such as the breathing or sitting meditations and the walking or body-scan meditations.

To continue on your journey, take a piece of paper and write a letter to yourself sharing where you are at this very moment in your life. Include what you want to remember from this book and what activities you want to keep doing as you move forward in your life. After you have written this letter, seal it in an envelope and date it for three months from now.

something more

After three months have passed, open your letter. When you reread it, reflect on where you are now. If you aren't doing what you wanted to be doing, you can start now. You might want to add to your original thoughts or change things based on your current life. Know that you can always write a letter to yourself to check in and keep reminding you of things in your life that you want to remember.

Gina M. Biegel, MA, LMFT, is a psychotherapist in San Jose, CA, who works with adolescents, children, and families. She adapted the mindfulness-based stress reduction (MBSR) program for use with adolescents, creating mindfulness-based stress reduction for teens (MBSR-T). A randomized control trial assessing the efficacy of this program showed significant results. Biegel is director of research for Mindful Schools and conducts workshops and conferences teaching MBSR to a variety of populations. Her audio CD, Mindfulness for Teens, is available online at www.stressedteens.com.